Situationship Bingo

Situationship Bingo

Cover design by Alex Aikido

Edited by Mila Cuda and Sarah Nwafor

Formatted by Pooja Mehra

I dedicate this to Black girls knowing their worth.

Lonely and alone are not always the same. Become good friends with yourself. Love yourself so that you know what it looks like when someone else does or does not.

Remember that love of oneself is a practiced action, not a destination.

Table of Contents

Is there still time for romance in the revolution?

Can you hold my hands
as the night sets in?

Can we meet the urgency
of survival with yearning?

I'd just like to know
if it's too late to fall in love.

Land in love.

Root in love.

Is it too late for you
to teach my lips
new languages for gratitude?

To get swept out to sea
as the rivers run muddy

and we relearn what it means
to water ourselves?

Is it too late for you to remind me
what this revolution is for?

To:	
Subject:	**Lessons in Love**
Cc:	**Bitterness**

Dear [title of latest distraction],

I hope that you are well. I have been made aware that you are romantically/sexually interested in me. This is very kind.

I regret to inform you that my heart is [gone white] [counterclockwise in my chest] [pinning for letters from my ex] and as a result, I am having difficulty with [breathing] [hemostasis].

That being said, I hope we can connect in the future. You seem [lovely] [like a lifeline] [an aversion].

If you are interested in being contacted when my heart [rights itself against my sternum] [remembers its rhythm] [forgets the ex], then please fill out the form below.

Thank you & Take Care,

Form: <u>Please Check All That Apply</u>

Please Check All That Apply

Hellscape / Location?

- ☐ Single and searching
- ☐ Wanting
    - ☐ simplicity

Relational Orientation?
- ☐ Single
- ☐ Dating
- ☐ Monogamous
- ☐ Polyamorous
- ☐ Polyamoraly-Monogamous
- ☐ Platonically
    - ☐ dating
    - ☐ life-partnered
- ☐ Singly platonic
- ☐ Platonically-singly-dating
- ☐ Sexually interested
    - ☐ romantically abbreviated
- ☐ Open
    - ☐ at the mouth
- ☐ Openly closed
    - ☐ at the heart
- ☐ Partnered to play
    - ☐ -ing with me
        - ☐ my time
        - ☐ my will to live.
- ☑ All the ways one can find themselves alone.

Conversation with Someone Being as Honest With You as They Are with Themself

I'm not even looking for something right now.

Like really. I'm so done with dating.
I am good with myself.
Just being with myself.

I love the nights alone
how long they feel.
The bills all in my name
all up to me. I love leaving
everything up to me.

Never asking for help.

It's just me on my own.
Singularly singled out

I love it!

I love being around
cute people without the feel
of a nicotine-level buzz to the brain.

That I can feel the blood around my heart
thicken with want under the gaze of another
and it's not a big deal.

Right?

We can just enjoy each other
and it's not that deep.

Right?

It doesn't have to mean anything.
It doesn't have to go anywhere.

And it's cute. I can keep it cute.
Can be just friends. Of course.

Friends are the ones who know you best
and that's what I'm really trying to focus on
knowing myself. Being known.

Being seen.
Seeing me through seeing you.

You see me right?

So I wonder if you had to choose
what kind of person would you say I
should be with?

If you had to choose.
Just if you had to.

Notes on Love [2017]

Sometimes I think I've had a crush on everyone I've ever met.
There's just so much beauty to notice
and I always notice because I care.
I fall in love because I care.
Which is kinda why I fall in love with everyone.
But also why I fall in love with everyone except for me.

I have decided to stop being boi-crazy

is what I would like to say
to the soft bend of the guitar players'
knees as they buoy up and down on the beat.

I would like to say this to the crook of the bass player's arms
as they cradle their instrument solid
in this crowd of eager listeners.

I would like to say this except
now I accept my purpose
is to be an instrument.

To be held that way–precious.

To have other people dance to the sounds
of my bliss strummed by a sweet player's rhythms.

I have decided to stop being boi-crazy.
And them-centered.
A femme-fanatic.

It's just that…it's so much fun
and I have so much work to do.

Ekphrasis for Galaxy by gggrimes

I was taught to aim for the moon
and look where I've landed–
the space between your legs
with stars in my eyes.

No rocket or shrapnel.
Just softness. Just *please, please. Oh, yes.*
and elevation.

You unzip. I pull
the hem of your corduroy
with my teeth.

Trace my lips across the cosmos,
plant wishes for shooting stars.

It rains from the heavens.
The night tastes of citrus

I Would've Let Jennifer Eat My Body Or The Directors Didn't Yearn Hard Enough.

Suppose we rewrite the movie.

Jennifer is Black.
Some shade of night.
Hair some curl or coil of snake.

Her lips as venomous.
Me twice as charmed.

I would've danced for her.
I would have understood,

Of course you killed my boyfriend baby,
You missed me. I missed you too, honey.

I would've let her take my heart
up against the wall.
On her pink duvet.
While holding hands
in the back of my mom's minivan.

I would have let her bite
into me like a Red Delicious.

Anything to feed her lust or need.
You look hungry, let me take care of you

Baby, I would have let her be my baby.
And birth herself in my body over and over.

I would have asked her to hold my hand
when she did it. I would've gasped

when she swallowed me,
and in my last breath smiled

at the sight of me spilled
over all of her.

I would've told her
You look so pretty.

What Sex...

Borrowing lyrics
from Broken Clocks by SZA

Wanted to be	Was	Is
A hug by the kitchen sink. Fresh flowers after work. White petaled peonies	A Tinder text. A plan for adulthood. A man–forgettable.	Infrequent. Available: uninteresting.
just blush in the center. Lush in the center gentle. Sweet. Full.	Disappointing. Cliché.	Longing for ways to be filled that haven't been invented yet.
You love me... *You love me.* *You love me!*	A longing and an ache.	

Reasonable Reasons to Fall in Love

1.) The uptilt corners of your mouth as I sing in the kitchen.

2.) I made boiled kale with vinegar and honey
(I was trying to experiment)
and you ate it anyway.

It's not that bad...okay well, actually...

then you proceeded to take small bites.

3.) The way you love my efforts as much as my success.

4.) To the question of picking me up from the airport
you said *I insist!*

5.) On a walk by the beach

6.) you pointed to a dog jumping towards the clouds.
Playfully toying with birds
and said *that one's me.*

7.) In the middle of an argument I try to change the subject
to which you respond *cool story*
(kinda mean but) thank you
for calling my evasion what it is–a story.

Thanks for helping me rewrite mine.

8.) You wiped tears from my cheeks.

10.) Your sweetness taught me
   it's okay to receive, to ask for more.

11) That I can leave when it's not enough.

Situationship Bingo

Picasso! Paint red flags green.	45 minutes late to the date that isn't a date.	They're *just friends* with their ex.	Being the more interesting half of your conversations.	They have *a lot going on**\n\n*note: anything that requires clarification can be considered *a lot going on.*
Intimacy beginning and ending at the closeness of your skin.	*I should get this for them!*	*I love you* before the first argument.	Speaking honestly only after you've swallowed spirits braver than you.	Butterflies! or Anxiety!
Checking your phone every two minutes for a text you won't receive for two hours or two days.	*They're soo cute!*\n\n(true)	Free Space! For your childhood.	Covertly checking their Instagram.	Underestimating your self-worth.
Random bouts of jealousy.	Making them a playlist.	Sex Fantasies.	They're *not into labels.*	Intense fear of dying alone.
Always texting first.	*Hey Siri! Play Why Don't You Love Me by Beyoncé.*	Thriving on Praise.	Canceling plans to make time for them. *Time for them* becoming Time.	Wanting. Wanting more.\n\nWishing you were enough.

Wherein I Try Not to Think About The Ex.

Sometimes I play this game with myself
where I put my pinky fingers in front of my eyes
and wave them back and forth
until it looks like a flesh-colored gondola.

The trick is to keep my gaze steady. Unblinking.
Fixed to the tip of my nose.
So here, it makes sense when my eyes start to water.

Here, it makes sense when the tears come.

Sarah Self-Disguises as a Cactus [2021]

I get all my nourishment from myself.

(I'm sooo chill!)

When you're not looking,
I satiate my thirst
and longing by looking
for you in the sun.

(I barely need any water!)

I drink all the dregs from the air
and soil. (*You can forget about me
for weeks!*) I parch everything
in my appetite for a sweet watering.

It still won't be enough.
I hold on to every drop for a dryness
that I know will inevitably come again
until the next time you come again.

I love you regardless.
Seem content.
Pretty. Vibrant.
Thick green skin.
What a glow! you'll say.

I'll survive. I'll be here (*no pressure!*)
You can come back
when you can (*and that means*
you'll always come back!)
But when you water me?
I can burst into a bloom.

When the care comes, with some consistency
I know it's safe to spare some energy
for this pink indulgence of a heart.

Maury, forgive me

I am the father
of my own toxicity.
It's true.

All the tests say
the common denominator
in my relationships
is me.

Damn.

What the hell we 'gon do now?

The mother parts of me are running
around the set screaming.

I'm so embarrassed.
I was always a good kid.
Straight A's for showing up.

Now look at me.

That's what happens when you introduce sex
to a god-fearing mind.

Let's pray for her
Everyone back home will say.

Everyone back home will say

Her mother   this.
Her father   that.

And so on and so forth.

Truth is?
It's not my parents
or the prayers.

It's that prayer works and I prayed
to be liberated from my mistakes
but never to avoid new ones.

I prayed to satiate my wanting
the best way I knew how.

And so here I am.

Crawling into and out of another emotional bed.
But it's so cozy here
Egyptian Sheets in these bad habits.

I'm so used to this bed
made up exactly how I laid it–
with temporary lovers to lavish
my fulltime loneliness and unspoken longings.

How can I get up and face the world now?
I heard it's cold and hard living in the truth.

Two and a Half Truths

We didn't separate–we took different cars
and coasts across the country.

I didn't cry my heart out–I was trying
to desalinate the ocean.

I wasn't jealous–I saw sunlight in your eyes
when you smiled at them and I wanted to feel warm.

You weren't lying–you were
watering resentment with your spit.

And I am exactly as I am
or would have been without you.

Goldilocks of Heartbreak

Ekphrasis for Mary J. Blige

Sounds the shade of navy blue tide my body
cracked against the shores of my grief.
Sleep don't come easy here…
nowhere…everywhere.

Time is sloshing *since you been away bo[i].*

Asphyxiating surender suspends me.
I wake finding that life *don't come easy*
that *my whole world is up!*-ended.

Floating and sinking at once
I have no idea of an ocean floor.

I'm so sorry sorry sorry.
Sorry! I haven't responded to that text
There's no reception in the deep.
Sorry! I canceled again–the anglerfish
and I have dinner plans swallowing
the salt tears *fallin' from my eyes.*

I settle into the sadness
ask Mary J–is the ocean too big on me?
She says *no.* It fits just right.

To:	My Therapist
Cc	
Subject	My lies always keep me awake

Hello Dr. [redacted],

I know it's 3:00 am and I should be asleep because we've been working on how I care for myself since the breakup. But we've also been working on the importance of honesty in the therapeutic relationship. And really what wins out–honesty or rest in a relationship?
Apparently, honesty because I'm finding that it's hard to sleep when I replay the day(s) in my head and the things I was or wasn't truthful about and so here I am.

Earlier today in session, you wondered if I'd *consider going back to* ███████ *if they asked* me? and I said no. Which is only half true. Because I would consider it. A lot.

I would consider it
as I accidentally come across their shirt in my clothes bin
and inhale their scent in the middle of the laundromat.
I would consider it
as I set aside the shirt from my wash pile, wishing
to wash nothing of them away.

I would consider it
at home as I cry with the shirt in hand before deciding that's enough
and folding it away. Just to unfold it again hours later.

I'd consider it as I repeat this cycle.

And then–I would say no.

I just felt the need to admit my whole-truths because I miss ███████ like
grief is an empty cup.
We know it's empty because we see the container. Without the container
it's nothing–just air.
And absence is not nothing. Grief is not nothing.

I know it's late, but I can't sleep until I tell you that I still miss them
because it's true.
I wish they could know that. I just feel like someone should know that.

After Maria Giesbrecht

I have a habit of holding on
to other people's habits. Particularly
those of the ones I've loved.

I always place my dad's order at restaurants
and I sleep with my grandmother's earrings
hoping to hear her in my dreams.
On long drives I listen to an old friend's
favorite podcast.

And as for you, today I'm hoping
to find you in the Trader Joe's frozen aisle
searching for the scallion pancakes
you cooked me over a California sunrise.

I no longer have the sunrise
nor the taste of it. It seems
they've discontinued them altogether.

Superstitious when ghosts
don't want to come home with me
I try not to cry in the car ride home.

Later that day when I can't tell
if it's the grief or grime of the city
that has belabored my lungs

imagine my smile when I find
the air purifier you gave me
waiting in the back of my closet.

Oh, you.

Imagine my smile at the memories
of kind offerings from your heart
and our tender care for each other.

When I find the air purifier you gifted me
I can't help but wonder about the winter
gloves I gave you in turn
and hope you still have them.

That in some timeline
I'm still holding your hands
and you are taking my breath away.

Conversation Between My Two Favorite Sex Toys

Nnenna has been…distant lately.
No?

                         Yes! Distant! SO distant! I was just
                                   going to say that.

….and we love Nnenna.

                                Of course. Love her!

Love the way she smells.

                           And the way they taste.

God, the way they taste.

                It's like this..
                Citrus sorbet!

                             Yes! Exactly that

Mmmm…ahem. Yes.
But it's like they're not even
here anymore.

                         And even when they are here
                     It's like they're somewhere else.

Right?

                   Do you think she's still not over ███ ?

Nooo, no way. It's been
so long.

                   Like SO long….but can I just say?

Say?

The sex was better
when they were around.

My goodness, so much better.
Not because of them

Of course not.

But because she finally gave
herself permission to feel herself.

And like, we love her.
LOVE her.

But it's like, when are you going
to love yourself?

Right! Like you can't be into yourself
just because someone else is into you.

Exactly! Like your pleasure
isn't just a placeholder for the next person
to break your heart!

Right? And like, she sleeps with
us every night.
But that's all we do is sleep.

Sometimes she'll pick one or
both of us up just to hold us
and it's the sweetest thing.

                                    So sweet! The wanting in her eyes.
                              The reflection of our phallic symmetry
                                          shining against her iris.

Her eyes look so dewy. Like
all the water between her legs
rushed to her head.

                              Exactly like that! And I can see all of it
                                        spilling through her lashes
                              Like she's so close to touching and then…

                              Nothing.

And then nothing.

                        …..

                                    Do you think she's avoiding us?

I think she's scared.

From The Woman Who Punched SZA in Her Broken Clocks Music Video

Borrowing lyrics from The Weekend by SZA

And she's over there talkin' 'bout–

My man is my man, is your man
heard it's her man too.

Can you believe it?

My baby?

I think actually the fuq not.

Hell yeah, I punched that bitch.
Left her ass cryin' on the outside
of the club where she belong.
Outside of a job to match her outside mind.

I mean, was I not clear?
That one is *mine*.

And yeah, yeah,
You can't own a person.
And *they don't belong to you.*

Okay?

They may not belong to me but our time did.
All the care I put into them does.
The life we crafted together does

And will.

And I understand
That people cheat because they want to.

Okay.

But that's me and they business.
I woulda' left her ass alone.
But then she came to me talkin'

I just keep [them] satisfied through the weekend
You like nine to five, I'm the weekend

Like, the fuq?
At that point it was just getting disrespectful.

If anyone's the weekend
I'm the weekend.

I am the joy
the play
the sanctuary
from a long week
the Sunday morning task
signaled with an R&B smooth.

I am the nourishing work.

It is a gift to love me.
To be loved by me.

And I tried to leave that bitch alone.
Even after she decided to fuq on someone
who don't belong to her.

Even tried to ignore her desperate
cause I know that side of the mirror too.
Know what it's like to be *fallin' all over love.*
To be wanting. Constantly.

To know what they need and hope
that giving it makes them need you back.

I know that side of the mirror.
And tried to be kind to the reflection.
I tried not to break my fingers on the glass.

But then she called me *nine to five.*
Called the work of loving me outside its' name
Something other than what it is–a gift.

She saw me standing in the rain
holding my heart and decided
to roll by just to splash me with the dirt
from the concrete.

And that was just too damn much.
Broke my pride.
So I broke her nose.

The Next Situationship Has to Fight Me at Dawn

Draw sword and duel my ass
at the top of a hill as the sun crowns
themself over the horizon.

I'm so serious.
I'm gonna suckerpunch you.
Mollywap you motherfucker.[1]
Play with me again.

Shiiit I might even shadowbox myself.

The way I keep giving out chances to niggas that don't exist
the play-pretends of people I make in my head.

How I jump into the air
and come up surprised that the asphalt burns
when I crash into the ground.

I'm over a fantasy.
Angel wings that don't exist
and holding out for dreams.

I'm gonna date someone regular.
An accountant.
A data scientist.

(Y'all know any dyke data scientists?)

Someone with a Roth ira?

---

[1] Please note: people that fight do not say "mollywap"

Who works with numbers
and their ability to provide exactitude?

See, I like my boxes neat.

Tidy. Reliable.
To show up at 10:45 if our date is at 11.
To wear pantsuits
and rulers in their pantsuit pockets.

I like a nigga who plans.
I'm tired of *go with-the-flow.*
And *I'm not into labels.*
Or *Let's live in the moment.*

Fuck that.
Which moment? What time?
I have my calendar out right now.
Save my name as Census Bureau in your phone
because I want a label for everything.
A category for every feeling.
A box for every hurt and storage units for every box.

I want a measuring stick for all the yards of distance
between your expectations and my loneliness.

I want the exact equation for safety
in the calculated risk of intimacy

I want a formula for the nausea-inducing hurt
in the aftermath of relational-loss.

I want to not care.

Like *actually* not care
or
I want to be in Love.

And if I fall for the imitation again
trick myself into the safety of a secured rejection

I'm gonna draw my sword
and run us both straight through.

Venus planet of love was destroyed by global warming– did its people
want too much too?
-Mitski

I too was called an earth once.
A home for some life

now unmoored
now wanting
now singular and watching
the cosmic waltz

between a new earth
and their moon.

Longing for a lunation of a lover
to look at me in their leisure.

Still–I'm not a victim.
Just a beggar.

Give me one good movie kiss.

It's enough. I'll love the story
in the absence of the teller.
Cup its' tale in my hungry hands
make it tall.

Reshape it like I have reshaped
my landscape for you again.
And again.

And still nobody wants me.

Saturn has 146 moons
and I must watch.

Prettiest girl at the party
with everyone to enamor
and no one to talk to.

Can cast a spell
and yet not one
that lets me into your orbit.

I inch toward the sun
and know the longing
will eviscerate me.

But damn the tides
let them rise drown
and then dry the life in me
if it means I will be of gravity today.

A captivating capture
of your attention today.

Did you see me?

Did I glitter?

Was I enough?

I Match with god On Tinder

G:...

Me:....

G: So, why'd you swipe right?

Me: It seemed kinda rude not to, to be honest lol.

G: Well, honest is nice. Thanks.

Me: So... is it as hard to meet people for you as it is for me?

G: Honestly? It's worse.

Me: Really?

G: Yeah.

Me: But you're kind of a big deal?

G: Yeah. So everyone wants something from me and no one wants me.
    Ya know?

Me: Yeah, I do know. I wish I didn't.

G:.. Real. So, do you want anything?

Me:.. I mean, yeah it'd be nice.

G: *sigh*

Me: YOU offered!

G:.. True, I did.

Me: Is it still okay? To receive I mean.
read: 8:58 am.

Sent: 10 pm
Me: I just checked my email!!

G: And?

Me: My Student loans were forgiven??

G: And?

Me: Someone bought my mom a house. 😭

G: You're welcome. 😎

Me: Thank you!! 🙏
Me: I will say, a response first would be nice, haha.
Me: I got nervous when you left me on read.

G: An action is a response.
G: So is an inaction.
G: Remember that for the people you're dating too.

Me: *sigh*

Me: I thought being a lesbian would be easier or...kinder
than this.

G: And I thought people would love me for giving them the world.

G: Now we're both disappointed.

Me: Why are you even on here anyway?

G: Same reason as you.
Just looking for some fun.

In which Chiron Responds

Where did you first learn to feel the shame
of wanting?

At the bottom of a river.

I remember | I imagine
my mother's teen self

finding private spaces to lactate and weep
for a baby she hoped would not come.

One is only as true as their origin story
and the truth is I'm scared
everyone will discover my secret
that I am actually unwanted.
am actually a terrible thing
an imposter.

An unlovable abandoned
at the bottom of the river
who through happenstance
found herself floating, carried
to the end of a wishing well.

That Apollo who shone on my newborn face
and Artemis who pulled me up with the tide
will love me only until they realize
they've mistook the magic of our meeting
with me.

That upon their realization I will drown
in their disappointment.

Is there freedom in being unknown?

I am not sure.
I know there is fear in being discovered.

People reveal who they are by what they show.
Can you open yourself up to listen?

I would not know.

I take people personally
but impermanently.

There were supposed to be flowers
After Jennifer Espinoza

at the altar where i would wait
for a h*sband
with a mom i spoke to
mooney-eyed of love.
there were to have been many dates.
where i had parents.
and the parents waited at the door for a nice bo[i]
with messy hair
and a sweet smile to pick me up.
the parents were to have said
have our daughter home by eleven
and *I'm watching you! She's precious you hear me!*
i was to have been precious. and precarious
in my fragility in ways which only a mother could see
i was supposed to have been seen. a seed
a sapling. watered precise in my stormy tantrums
a teen. coming home sobbing
i was to have slammed doors
and thundered. and rained.
shape-shifted moods
And *mom, you don't understand*
i was to have been young.
instead–i grew. and i mourn
all the bad decisions i did not make.

instead. my house was quiet
without worry for *such an old soul*
so mature for her age

i did my homework
i got straight A's
i was captain of…
president of…
my mother's sunshine
a weeping willow bowed to my parents pride
a daughter-shaped hollow where a spirit ought to be
and i wonder what renditions of rebellion
and rapture my teen self would have had
what curfews broken. fights flung. skirts shortened.
questions kissed had she known
there were to have been parents protecting her mistakes
had she known
that making one did not make her one.
and what a fantastical find it is to happen upon the lush green
between who you were and who you will be. I wonder
who i would've been. had i been allowed my mistakes
my growth. my tending. what flowers you'd see
in my garden.

Lesbian Grieving

I

When I was a kid, after watching *Fresh Prince of Bel Air*,
I asked my mom if women look different after they have a baby.

She said, *yes. Sometimes.*
and so I thought this was the reason
Aunt Viv looked different after season three–
because she had a baby.

I was young and had not yet realized
the real reason (colorism)
so I thought that's what it meant to grow up–

that one day I also would wake with a different body.

That I could be
Ashley Banks
or Beyoncé
or whoever my mother was.

That women would swap lives with me like dolls.

The way they did Aunt Viv.

II

A recurring dream.

On a date. Us. In a bar. Dimly lit. Hand
draped on my thigh.
A smirk. A hairflip. Myself

backless low necked dress
the color–a shimmering midnight.

Them: full-bodied. Like me.
Them: Skin–a shade of deep earth.

We dance and I trip.
In my heels.
Since when do I wear heels?
I try to flip my hair to a casual recovery

but I catch stiff ends.

I haven't felt my scalp crack
under formaldehyde creams
since seventeen and yet I tug the ripped wool of my strands.

Then I remember–

this performance always looks better on the model.

III
A recurring dream.

Man. Woman. Walk
down the street. Arm in arm
woman: notices a baby. Smiles.
man's eyes widden.

Woman: looks down toward brown palms
mine? I am a –

retake: swap out the man for an asterisk
retake: swap out the baby for a question
retake: swap out my hair for a silk press
retake: swap in Beyoncé

retake. Retake. Re-
take the film–broken. Just me
on an empty set smoking a cigarette.
Posturing for photos

trying to look cool for Tinder.

IV
A family dinner–watching a wh*te woman
on tv pretend to be a princess.

They went to finishing school, you know.
Very classy. I would have liked to go.
Says my mother, to my sister and I.

My sisters and I grew up watching wh*te girls
be princesses. Watching wh*te girls allowed love
even if they decided to be something else.

Of all the stories we studied
Anne was my favorite–I too liked to disappear
into a daydream.

My sister and I were so young

only knew how fun it was
to play pretend–the tea sets.
The heels. The hair. The blonde.

But silver spoons are difficult
to eat fufu with–I prefer my hands.

I prefer women
who prefer their hands
caressed in palm oil.

My mother calls Elizabeth Taylor
a classic beauty, while I
lick the greasy red from my fingers.

I'm Moving to California Where Aloneness Makes Sense
After Danez Smith

I'm tired of the sky's sunless indifference.
Of the concrete and the silver high buildings
no one can afford to live in
all shades of gray but so sexless I couldn't choke
on the steely cool of it even if I tried.

I'm tired of trying
on heavy puffer coats
and walking in seas of people
whose pupils I haven't seen in months.

I'm moving to California

where being alone is the brave artistic choice of becoming
instead of the poor consequence of conditioning.

I want to go where a lack of reach
is attributable to miles of distance a country's width apart
instead of an arm's stretch toward the phone.

I'm going to California
where I can cry about leaving home
under a palm tree.
With a mimosa.

Where I can drive to the beach
and let my saltwater eyes reacquaint with the ocean.

No one is swimming in Boston city's swamp-waters.

Someone would notice.

Notes on Love

> *Venus planet of love was de-*
> *stroyed by global warming*
> *-Mitski*

I don't mind being remade.

People have burned for less noble gods
and I am just a human

who longs to do what humans do–Love.
Worship.

I Go to The Club to be Held

It is Pride in the Oakland side of East Bay
and I am abandoning propriety.

I am ripping off my chamomile colored cardigans
and donning my nipple covers
my black leather skirt sitting just above my ass.

I am dancing tonight.

At the club, lights bend lilac
in neon hues. I am washed royal
while Queen Whitney sings through the speakers.

I too, *wanna dance with somebody*
who loves me [?]

It's a question I've always wrestled
with and like prayer or practice
a deep-brown gender queer being appears.

I smile.
They smile back.

I ask them to dance
They say yes.

Then punctually the music changes
to a spanish guitar, twirling rhythms
and the summer breeze under our skirts.

I place my hand where theirs is waiting to meet mine.
I want to say, *thank you for holding me today.*
Insead, I slide my other hand across their shoulder
and feel their cotton cloth caress me.

I nest my head in the crevice of their neck
just for this dance.

We are hugging on the dance floor
irregularly intimate.

They rock me like a child
and who knew we could heal
mother wounds at the club.

Put intimacy where it's been out.

Use legs for joy
outside opening.

I am admittedly bitter
at lovelessness.
at the world.

but for the moment
the world is in these arms
a gentle sway.
And for now the question–*who loves me[?]*
has an answer–*somebody.*

For now it's enough.

My sister

a reluctant participant
in my queer shenanigans
cuts my hair.

Or more accurately
she hears the shear of sharp scissors
through my coils cascading to the floor

and asks from the other room
what are you doing?

To which I respond
Nooothing… hehe.

And just like that we are ten and five years old again
and I have inevitably gotten into something
which she must inevitably help me clear up.

Only this time what I've gotten into
is myself.
Is mess.
Is depression.
Is post-graduation-deep-pandemic times.

What I've gotten into
is the *20-somethings*
and I can't figure out how to get out.
Or get on.
Or fall in love

or love back
or pay my phone bill
or do my taxes.

Or leave my ex.

So the best I can do
is scissors to hair.
Is weight from scalp
hopefully from my mind too.

Hopefully with a shorter sheer
the breeze might whisper
sense into me.

And my sister doesn't really understand
my queerness
why I'd cut off my hair
why I love the people I do

But she does understand siblinghood.

Does understand grieving.
Does know a five-year-old trying to try
something for the first time
and knows that the birthright of our young
is help in the absence of parentage.

So with a sigh and Virgonean perfection
she takes the scissors from my hand
and helps me shed.

The Voice of Monaleo Calls to Get Me Together.
Borrowing lyrics from Flush 'Em

Hold on, no way you thought [they] was the one?

I really hoped.
But I knew.

No way you was puttin' out, puttin' out, puttin' out
ain't break the nigga for nothin'?

Leo, it's hard for Black grls.
For sapphic Black grls.
Grls whose grlhood was always a wanting.

Waiting for affirmation that does not come
and then I saw them.

Tasted their small sweetness
and confused crumbs for the cake.

Thought if I was good and patient
I'd feel full with all the Love they'd fill me
and so I waited for it.

And waited for it.

Waited for them to be
worth waiting for.

Dummy.

Yeah… yeah.

What have I taught you?

That I deserve sweetness like honey
not just sugar.

What have I taught you?

That someone who acts like they don't care
about me ain't actin'

that choosing myself doesn't have to feel good
to be good for me.

Right! Nice hoes comin' in last.

Now, I'm not sure if–

Nice hoes comin' in last!

Okay maybe that's true Leo!

Maybe at the end of the night
No one is giving me sainthood
for giving the most.

No one is calls me divinity
for depleting myself.

But fuck, Leo, are the most revered women
not always martyrs? Or mothers?
And I always wanted to be revered.

Leo, there are few examples of Black grls
like us and I'm not sure who to be without them.

What have I taught you?

…That I still have the years
and time ahead of me to find out

If I don't waste it.

What have I taught you?

That I can be my own affirmation and best thing.
I don't have to wait for crumbs
to make this life-shit my cake.

What have I taught you?

That a shower of love can't turn
And turn poop to potpourri

To flush em' instead

Yeah, wipe them tears, pussy.

Time heals everything, I don't need anything. Hallelujah...
-Beyoncé Giselle-Knowles Carter

The truth is, there will probably be no reconciliation.
So I am trying to pray instead.

because *I just, I need to [move] through this*
and the only actions I can care for are my own
is what my therapist says.

And because the expectations have failed me
and Bibles have failed me
I am repeating much
of what my therapist says these days.

There will probably be no reconciliation.
Still, I can't stop saying *probably*
to dead things and ashen-bridges.

I'm so sad. I have time.
Time heals everything
and I'm trying not to drown
mine in movement.

Time can be a thorough debridement
if I let it cleanse me, *hallelujah.*

I have nothing left of my past
I don't need anything to follow me
into my present.

With few friends
and long roads ahead
I am frugal these days
with my time, my investments, myself

I don't need anything
time heals everything
and so I savor my hours slowly.
Take a long bus ride instead of a lyft
though it is raining. I savor that too.
I pray to her and let the drench
accompany me home.

I let my tears build hotly. Fiercely.
And fall gentle.

Hallelujah, I'm letting things go.

Love is about Building the Fire, Not Running Into It
Notes from Aries Venus

Today I learn how to build a fire.
I learn the difference between the short spark
of tinder and the endurance of fuel.

Like a Priestess of Vesta tending
the life flame of their maiden goddess,
fuel can sustain a fire for as long as there is focus.
Diligence. Dedication.

Sacrifice–fire demands
the driest and deadest of me
as kindling in exchange for a phoenix' flight.

So I practice. So I feed
and feed and flame sparks to life
off of old memories.

Photos of ex best friends.
Letters from people I don't speak to
CD's. Certificates. Versions of myself
I have no business carrying
across the years of my life.

To Love is to transmute
is setting alight attachments
to who I was if it means I can be
true to who I am now.

Fire demands The Now.

So I watch what I thought
was my life shapeshift to smoke and smolder.

My hands are empty and I'm scared
because as an earthbody I thought holding on
to what I can grab would keep me rooted
 in the midst of change. I didn't realize
it would also keep me rooted in the past.

Fire swallows death
in the face of fear tells me that Love
is about building a fire and surrendering to it.

Is risking the vulnerability to start over and over again
and the humility to remember I know nothing
each time Love makes me reborn.

Fire teaches me Love in the present
by being in it we're already changed by it
and isn't that good?

And isn't that god?

When Sadness Persists at the Dawn of Spring

I'd like you to know the ache in your chest
is habitual and cyclical. I don't care to be good
at forgetting so remember to go outside today and tomorrow.

Even in the cold.

We may be sad again
but it's very likely that the sun will be out.

Or I may see another cardinal sometime
and the vibrant red will gash my heart open beautifully.
In a way which levies the wind
and pigments flight.

Do you remember how the air holds your lungs?
Tenderly. In each palm.
If you forget, which is very likely, breath begins usually after chest-
fall.

When plummeting please remember
the only difference between a yellow butterfly and a falling leaf
is simply the temperature of the day.

I'd like to prepare you for your first heartbreak
but as soon as we pass through one lightless threshold
we're born, and born again, and forgetting
is so easy when there's so much I'm dying to see.

Eventually we stop trying to give the sadness a name and assignment
and the song is sung without the memory of them
and red becomes just red without all the plumage.
But what's the point in roaming without a place to rest?

Let's see what life can be molded
from the pieces of your last one on the ground–
I have a friend who once made a beautiful church-window out of mir-
rors and sea-glass.

I'd like to prepare you for your first heartbreak
but life is ravenous
so instead, let me just teach you how to sing.

After June Jordan

I am no longer settling for a chase
painting red flags green
unclear boundaries
from myself
or others
lying to myself
or from others
ignoring my own needs
in the hopes that someone else
will validate what beauty
I know to be true about me.

What I know to be true about me–I will be

a ghost to inconsistency
a dial tone to poor communication
a wall to porous boundaries
a holy verse to deception

and a great Love in the face of great Love.

I will be nobody's fool.
Least of all, my own.

A Lesbian Praise Hymn

And Lorde said
Women who want without needing are expensive and sometimes
wasteful, but women who need without wanting are dangerous-- they
suck you in and pretend not to notice.
(Zami 1:12).

Dear godexx
divinity
my ancestors
spirit guides

Let there be nothing scarce about me.
May I Love because I do
not just because I want to be Loved back.

Please lead me
out of heterosexism
but in tune with a grlfriend
or boifriend
or theyfriend.

Godexx, may we spend time
on farms more
and screens less
except for when watching
Sapphic Stories.

May the care we show each other
make hearts feel featherweight.

Goddexx, being a lesbian
I realize all the sweetness I crave exists.
I don't have too much want
Patriarchy has too little give.

Spirit, I don't want my
future boyfriend, theyfriend, grlfriend
to live at a distance.

They're already so far
I haven't seen them yet.

But, if this person and I do
have to be rivers apart
I won't complain much.

As we know Love knows no time.

A thirty-six hour drive
is a two hour flight
which is a day trip.

Thank you for this sexuality
that lets me bend time
by the hinge of a plane ticket.

I was taught a thousand years
is a day in heaven so I know god
is also a dyke.

Godexx and ancestors
I get so full my heart won't stop spilling over
on our Love.

May love fill me so I am able
to share the extra with someone
who doesn't make the excess run down my cheeks
someone who leaves cheek-kisses instead.

May I do as Love
because I want to
not just because I want
to be Loved back.

May I be Loved back regardless

Iséee!

Nnenna Comes out as a Rose Bush [2024]

Friends. Foes.
Larvae and winged creatures alike.

I know you all thought
I was a cactus. At first I did too!

(The thorns are easy to mistake
with my cousin's quills).

But after weathering storms with myself
receiving the rain and the bloom
in the aftermath of the skies's showers

I have realized that I am
in fact a rose.

I know. Quite a change.
But a magnificent one.

So let's try this again.

Hi! Nice to meet you!
My name is Rose / hip
Pronouns are thorne / thistle
and I am so excited to be blooming
with you!

If you deserve it.

Which brings me to my next point–
watering.

I know I had said the inconsistency
works for me but it turns out
that it does not.

If you want to see me flower
I need water. With consistency.
Or I will wilt.

I need sunlight.   Or I will wilt.
I need trimmings.   Or I will wilt.
I need the space to unfurl myself.   Or I will wilt.

Basically I need my needs
to be met as non-negotiables
instead of convenient crumbs
or I will wilt.

But don't get me wrong. There's nothing fragile about me.

35 million years of my lineage have sown seeds
that have weathered the weather of Earth's tantrums
I am resistant to even the most ravenous jealous spore.
I am if nothing else a survivor-dying brave in the winter
daring to live again in the spring.

I am nothing if not resilient
I just don't want to have to be.

Blooms are curated
only as vividly as the care put into them
and I would so love to open for you.

Unfurl my velvet petals
let you pet the scent of me
with your wandering nose
Sweet honeybee nourish yourself
with my dewy gospel.

But only if you know how to praise
How to offer. How to let me rest.
Ease open. Safe in the consistency
of a kind heart and steady pour.

Otherwise, all you will have is my thorns
and I will have your blood.

For the Black grls

After Ariana Brown

I want you to know that you are loved.

If not visibly then certainly
by all the invisible.

By the ancestors whose life
lives in you, whose bodies became
part of the soil that nourishes the clay of you
by the Earth who holds you
by the waters which baptize your feet.

You are loved by so much
and disrespected by a loud few.

Do not let a loud callousness
interrupt the daily quiet care
of all the life that sustains you.

You are loved
and deserve to be.

You deserve to be read to
to be prayed over
to be praised
to receive a raise
to take time off
to rest. You deserve
intention and attention paid

to your needs. Bills paid as you need
groceries bought and delivered.
You deserve dinners cooked for you
dishes done when you get home
floors swept and cinnamon
over every entryway you enter.
You deserve to enter as you are.
You deserve your own room
and room to breathe
room to make mistakes and try again
to be held gently with firm hands and patients palms
You deserve Love.
You deserve Love.

My love, you deserve Love.
It is your birthright.

A Tarot Reading Where I Hear Everything I Need to.

Ahh yes, okay you will get that job!
The one that pays you a lot of money for very little effort
and leaves you plenty of free time to frolic.
Plenty days of frolicing ahead of you.

All the stress you feel in your body?
Like a constant electric humm? It's all part of the plan.
It's to make you magnetic so you can attract
all the opportunities that serve you
and repel the ones that don't.

What else do the cards say?

Hmm...you will fall in Love again.
I'm sorry, I don't think it will be with [the ex].
The cards say you're going to cry a lot about this.
You're already crying a lot about this? That's okay!
The cards say it will get better.

The cards say sadness doesn't mean
you're not moving fast enough.
The pause that it offers is a recalibration.

In the cards, I see that this is uncomfortable for you?
Mmm, yeah that's right. I feel it more strongly now.
The Empress reversed and then again upright.

The cards say to have more fun being uncomfortable.

To get used to not knowing what you're doing
But that it feels right to be doing it.
The cards say to follow what feels right
and when nothing feels right do nothing, and see if that feels right.
And if that doesn't work go inside and feel for what feels wrong.

The cards say that what's hard for you
is not what's wrong with you
is often the very lesson for you to be learning.

The cards say get more sleep!
And drink more water!
Do not put your needs on pause
for another person. Look
at the pauses of your body as part of the creative process.

The cards say the needs of your body are not a luxury.

This has been a long reading
and the cards need rest now.

When you next need them
the cards will be with you.

Maybe Moving on is as Simple as Letting Paint Dry

On the eve of my move to California
I blotch the walls white as canvas
ready to be colored again by a new live-in.

I know this is not erasure of my past
but a ceremony for beginnings.

I laid the masking tape and tarp.
I moved the sheets and sat my bed
in the center of the room.

I emptied the room of memories
to make space for this.

I washed the walls gently
and said a prayer for the change.
I took down the art that reminds me of them
and said *thank you* to every ghost.

This is not avoidance of my past.
This is a cord cutting in service of new starts.
In service of my security deposit
of earthly futures to invest in.

I've cried so much in this room.

I've loved and made love to
in this room.

I've yearned and unlearned
my silence in this room.

I've loved you and said goodbye.
Now the finish is just around the corner.

I pick up my brush and paint.

Please Don't Bring your Last Ex to This Date

Blah, blah, blah trauma.

Blah, blah, blah heartache.

Blah, blah, blah grief.

Yes, I was loved and was left
and sometimes not loved well.

But we're here aren't we?

Ghosts are so persistent but I think they're jealous.
They're not alive like you and me.

I'd like to make my past
jealous of my present and future.

I want all the deadnames to stay dead.

Because of course, if a person couldn't Love me then
how will pouring their name out resurrect me now?

I'm not Lazarus. And my ex was not a miracle.

I don't want cling to the comfort of a known past
or avoid the uncomfortable unknown of the future.

Unknown is simply the symmetry of *potential*.
 Can we please explore ours?

And not talk about star signs like we know each other?

Oh a Taurus! Like my last [insert ghost here]
or
Ohh that is sooo [insert ghost here].

Can we please act like we're new here
in this beginning?

Can we act like we have the choice
to choose the shape of Love?
Instead of the ghosts of our grief?

Can we enjoy Love long enough before fear
of its loss? Introduce ourselves new?

I'll start. Hi, I'm a mirror.
I'm honored to see
such a beautiful reflection.

Acknowledgements

I give thanks to the kind benevolent ancestors of my matrilineal lineage. Daluu, I am a storyteller because of you/us. I am me, because we are us.

Thank you to my editor Mila Cuda! You are such a phenomenal poet. Our friendship and artistic collaborations are a shining example of the power Venus-ruled beings bring to this world. Thank you for helping me share my gifts.

Thank you Plantin Magazine for publishing *Goldilocks of Heartbreak.* Thank you Voicemail poems for publishing, *From The Woman Who Punched SZA in Her Broken Clocks Music Video.* Thank you Beestung Magazine for publishing, *Situationship Bingo,* though it was titled differently at the time. Thank you all for believing in my work and me!

Thank you mother earth, moon mother, and the sweet intimacy of my bedroom for holding all my tears, secrets, and rebirths so that I could conjure these poems.

Last, but not least, thank you to the Black women hip-hop artists and hip-hop feminists who inspired the ideas of this collection. Thank you for reminding me to remember my worth and then add tax.

With gratitude, I close this journey and this book. I lift this gratitude up to Spirit that it may rain down on us again, and again. Iséeee!

Biography

Sarah "Nnenna Loveth" Umelo Uzoma Nwafor (they/she) is a queer Igbo poet, performer, and facilitator. Their work explores Black g*rl-hood, Black queerness, Igbo Cosmology, Sensual play and rituals of healing. Nnenna published their debut chapbook, *Already Knew You Were Coming*, with Game Over Books in January of 2022 . They have also been featured on Button Poetry, WBUR's ARTery, VIBEs Magazine, and Ujima #Wire. When Nnenna is not writing, they are somewhere being romanced by the intensity of life. When they speak, their ancestors are pleased. Please follow their work on IG @pleasure.as.compass or at pleasurearthealing.com